HOW TO MAKE MEN HAPPY!

by TONI COFFE

First published in Great Britain by
Pendulum Gallery Press
56 Ackender Road, Alton, Hants GU34 1JS

© TONI GOFFE 1997

HOW TO MAKE MEN HAPPY
ISBN 0-948912-36-7

PRINTED 1997

All rights reserved. No part of this publication may be reproduced or transmitted in any form or by any means, electronic or mechanical, including photography, photocopying, recording, computer scanning, tracing, projecting, drawing from, painting from, torn out and framed or any information storage and retrieval system, or for a source of ideas without permission in writing from the publishers.

Printed in Great Britain by
UNWIN BROTHERS LTD, OLD WOKING, SURREY

HOW TO MAKE MEN HAPPY by TONI GOFFE

What, at first, might seem a **MISSION IMPOSSIBLE** on reflection maybe way off the mark. How To Make Men Happy, as so many women have found, is surprisingly simple.
Where a woman is like a complicated computer that has to be handled with very great care and sensitivity, a man just has an **ON** and **OFF** switch. Just switch him on and watch him go!

The only thing about this that women should remember is that YOU'VE GOT TO MAKE IT LOOK LIKE THE MEN THOUGHT OF IT FIRST. Once that is in their minds you can do anything with them.
There is another item to remember and that is to keep on telling them HOW WONDERFUL THEY ARE. You can keep on doing this for ever and they still believe you! It is like driving a car from the back seat, and steering him in the direction you want him to go.

Some men may catch on to you at this point and think you are trying to change them, but just say that you're not and go on and change them. Very simple really, just keep half a step ahead and you'll be OK.

Now the question of how to make them happy. They just want sex and to be looked after like their mothers did. You also have to let them play with the other boys down the pub, so they can reassure themselves that everything is OK. If the same thing is happening to the other men that is happening to them then everything must be OK.

If anything goes wrong with this and one of the men is showing signs of any independent thinking, just have a quiet word with his woman who will soon get him to toe the line.

LOOK AS IF YOU UNDERSTAND WHAT HE IS TALKING ABOUT....

TELL HIM ABOUT YOUR DAY....

LET HIM HAVE SOME OF HIS WAGES....

LET HIM WATCH T.V....

LET HIM DRIVE THE CAR....

LET HIM PLAY GOLF....

LET HIM PLAY WITH YOUR CAR....

LET HIM HAVE A SAY IN IMPORTANT MATTERS...

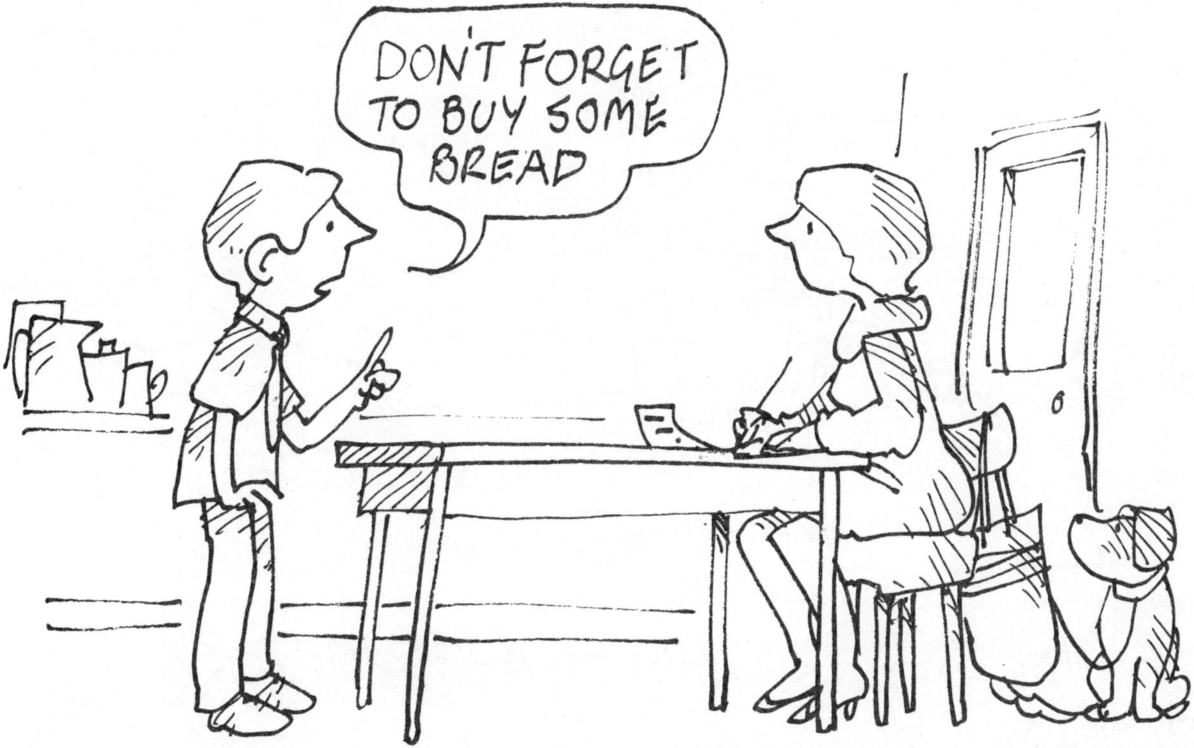

TAKE HIM OUT FOR A TREAT....

...LET HIM STEER THE SUPERMARKET TROLLY....

MAKE HIM APPRECIATE YOUR COOKING...

LET HIM DO THE COOKING NOW AND AGAIN....

LET HIM HAVE THE T.V. REMOTE CONTROL.....

"THANKS, BUT WE DON'T HAVE A T.V"

GIVE HIM LITTLE JOBS AROUND THE HOUSE...

"IT'S NOT JUST THE DUSTING YOU ENJOY IS IT?"

INTRODUCE HIM TO YOUR GIRLFRIENDS...

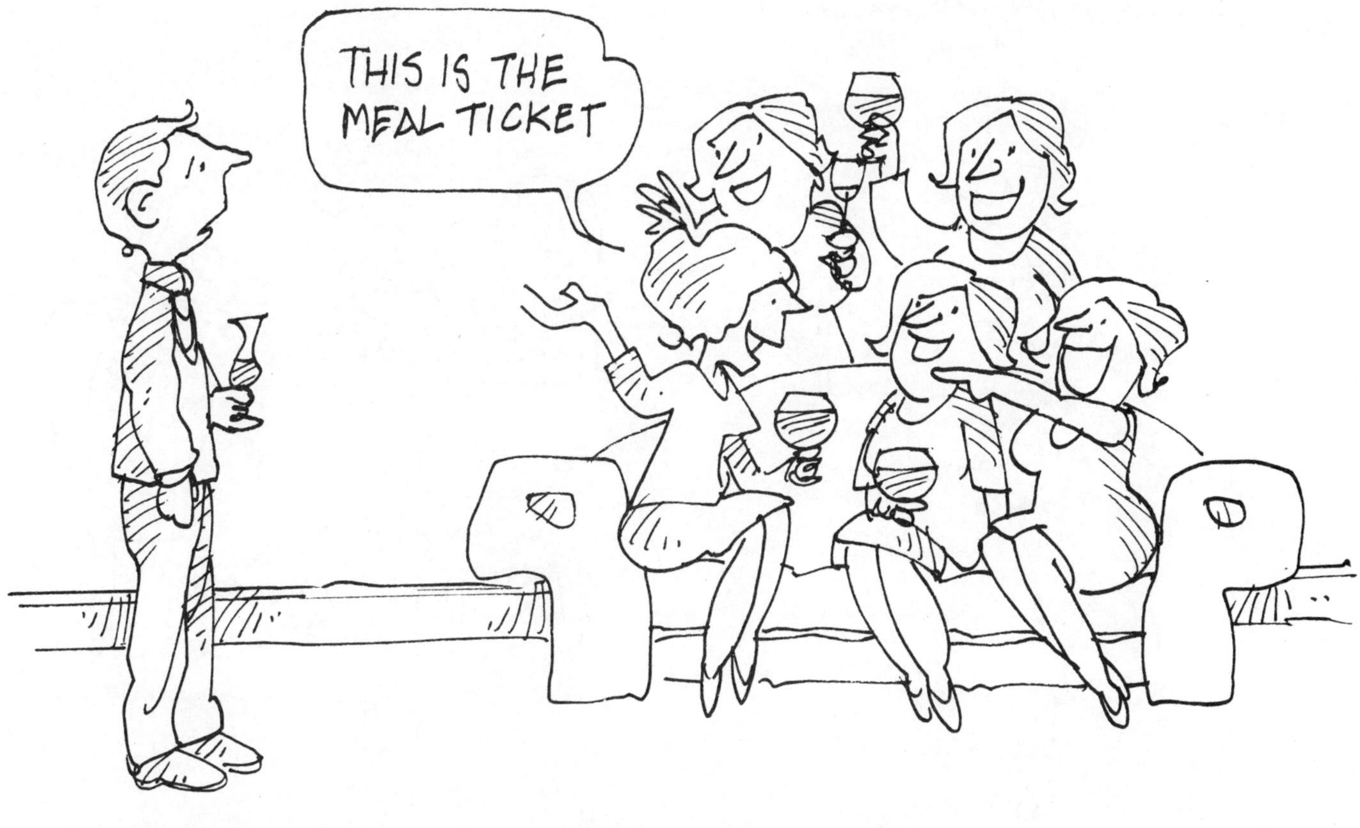

LEND HIM TO YOUR FRIENDS TO DO ERRANDS....

LET HIM BE ON HIS OWN SOMETIMES....

LET HIM HAVE HIS FREEDOM.... BUT NOT TOO MUCH....

LET HIM TAKE YOU OUT TO A RESTAURANT....

LET HIM PAY THE BILLS....

"THANKS"

LET HIM PLAY WITH THE CHILDREN....

LET HIM PLAY WITH HIS TOYS....

"FIVE MORE MINUTES, THEN OFF TO BED"

TELL HIM HIS D·I·Y IS GREAT!

"YES IT'S GREAT! IT'S A BLOODY GREAT HOLE"

TAKE HIM FOR WALKS....

"IT WILL MAKE YOU HAPPY..."

BUY HIM A PET TO KEEP HIM HAPPILY OCCUPIED....

"YOU LIKE LONG WALKS DON'T YOU?"

GO JOGGING TOGETHER ....

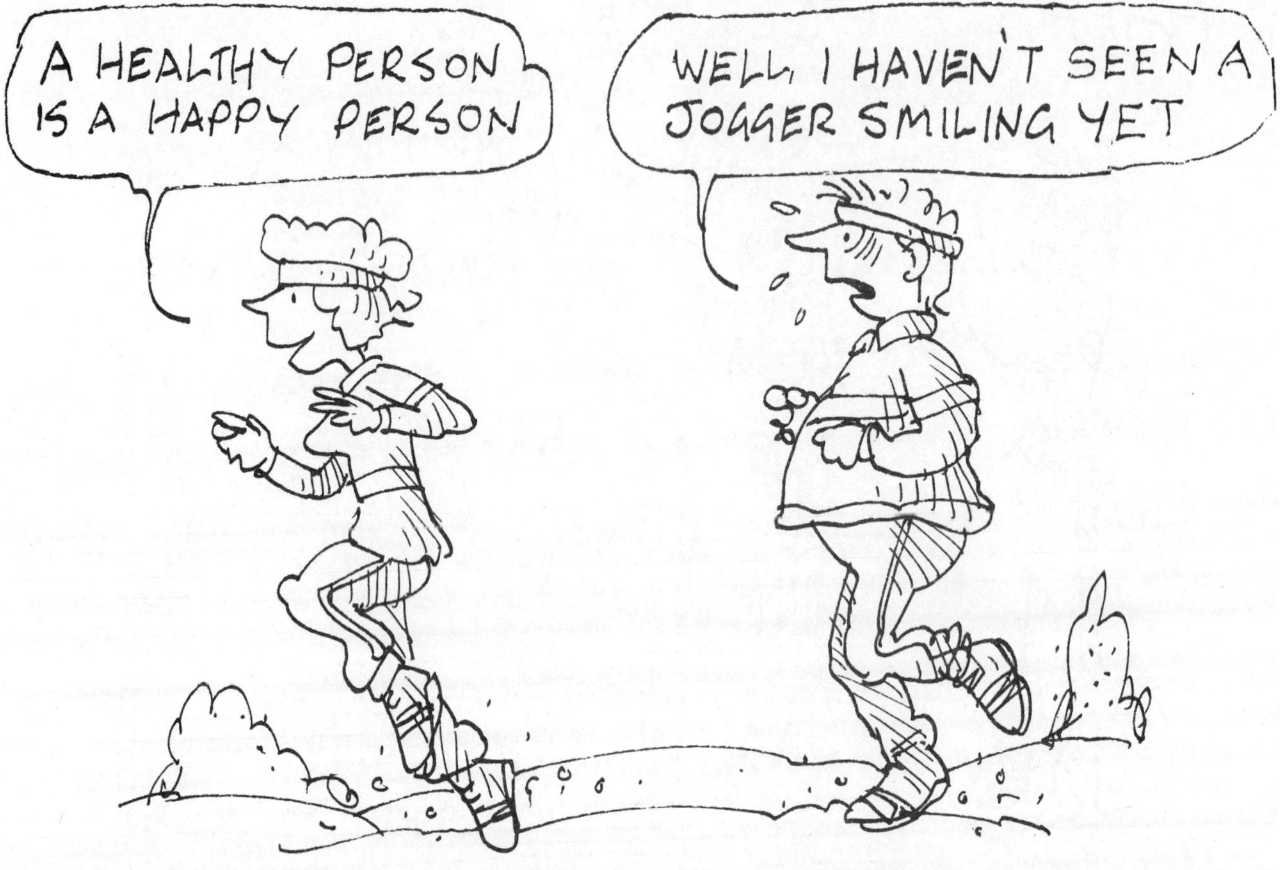

LET HIM WIN AT TENNIS....

"OH DEAR ANOTHER POINT TO YOU"

PLAY GOLF WITH HIM....

OH, NO, NOT ANOTHER HOLE-IN-ONE, THIS IS EASY

LET HIM PLAY ON YOUR COMPUTER....

"WHAT'S THE PASSWORD?"

"MALE MENOPAUSE"

ENCOURAGE HIM....

"HUM, NOT BAD FOR A MAN"

SAY SOMETHING 'NICE' TO ENCOURAGE HIM IN HIS ENDEAVOURS.....

"YOU'RE A TYPICAL SAMPLE OF THE MALE SPECIES"

"THANKS"

BUY HIM SOMETHING FOR HIS FISH POND....

"FEEDING TIME..."

LET THEM WASH UP, IT MAKES THEIR HANDS SOFT FOR TOUCHING YOU LATER....

"ANOTHER HOUR WILL DO IT"

ENCOURAGE FOREPLAY BEFORE SEX....

LET HIM HAVE SEX WITH YOU...

"OK, READY WHEN YOU ARE I SUPPOSE"

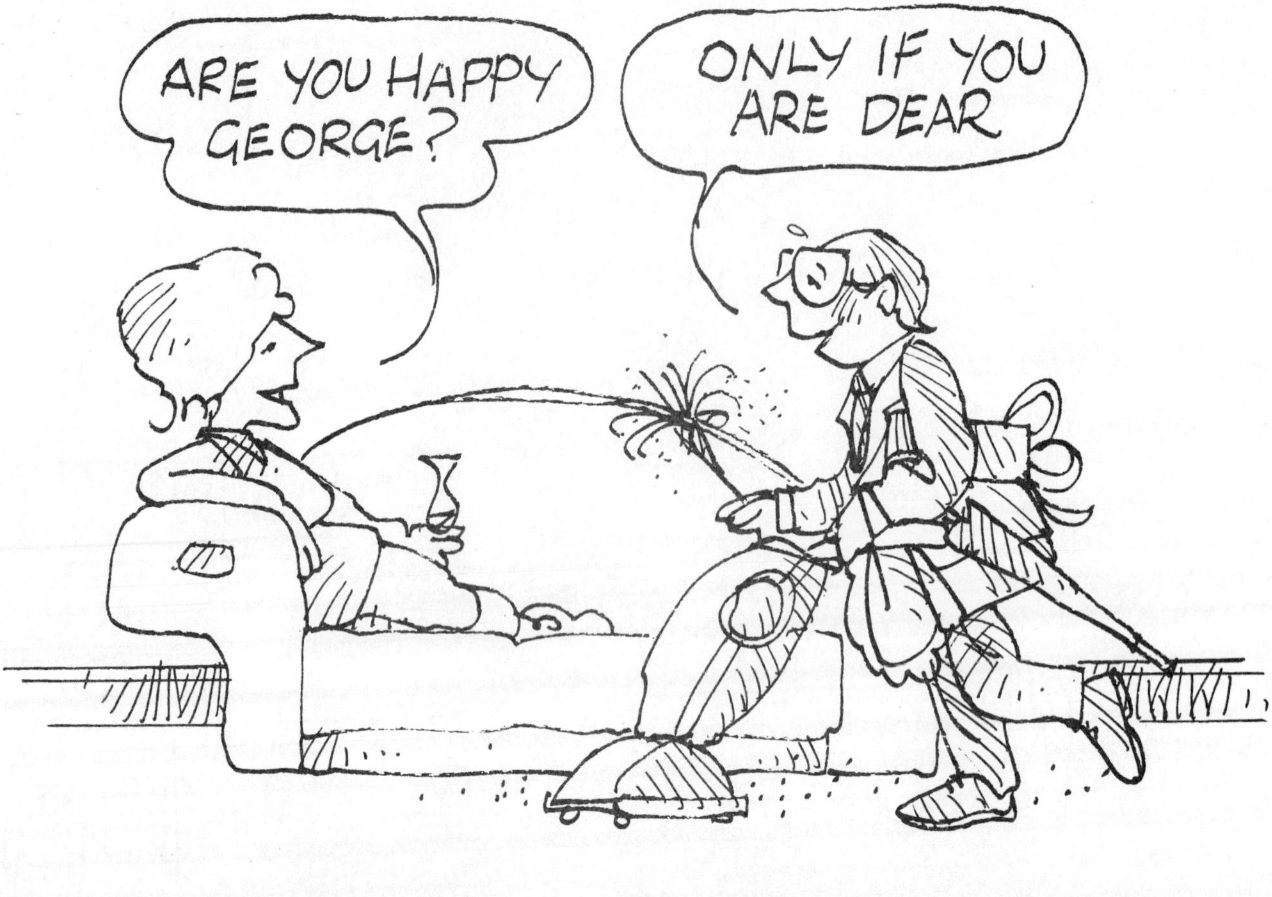
ARE YOU HAPPY GEORGE?
ONLY IF YOU ARE DEAR